# Sayings

## on

## Love

*Cheers!*
*David*
*Jones.*

Edited by
David C. Jones

Detselig Enterprises Ltd.

Calgary, Alberta, Canada

Sayings on Love, © 2000 David C. Jones
Cataloguing Information in Publication
Main entry under title:
Sayings on love
ISBN 1-55059-196-7
1. Love - Quotations, maxims, etc. I. Jones, David C., 1943-
PN6084.L6S39 2000 808.88'2 C99-911115-9

Detselig Enterprises Ltd.
210-1220 Kensington Rd. N.W., Calgary, AB T2N 3P5
Phone: (403) 283-0900/Fax: (403) 283-6947
temeron@telusplanet.net, www.temerondetselig.com

We acknowledge the financial support of the Government
of Canada through the Book Publishing Industry Development
Program (BPIDP) for our publishing activities.

ISBN: 1-55059-196-7 /SAN: 115-0324/ Printed in Canada
Cover design by Dean Macdonald

Portions from *A Course in Miracles,* copyright 1975, 1999,
reprinted by permission of the Foundation for A Course in
Miracles - 1275 Tennanah Lake Road - Roscoe, NY 12776-5905.
Citations are from the second edition.

# Introduction

Love is the ancestor of all spiritual values. It gives birth to them, and then is energized and vitalized by them; it incubates them, and then is magnified and immortalized through them. It does this with qualities like patience, persistence, happiness, courage. It joins with what it has already created, and in the process it receives back the life it gave — just as you receive love, loyalty and trust by giving them to others.

Patience, persistence, happiness and courage are all offspring of love, but they also enable and invigorate love. Love is sharing, and it must share to be itself. It needs its own creations; it needs them to interact with in order to flower — just as teachers need students in order to evolve. Without people to help us as we help them, we are all sterile and incomplete.

Patience is a daughter of love, and love desperately needs this child — because without patience, love has no time. It has no time for those who need time to develop, to unfold, to adjust, to see the light. It has no time for the slow, the insecure. No time for those who are not ready for instruction. Without patience, you, who are love's potential, will become irritable, intolerant, angry, demanding, selfish and short-tempered. Without it, you cannot be kind to yourself (the impatient can absolutely savage themselves!) Without it, you cannot even listen – and to listen is the first obligation of love.

Persistence is another child that love desperately needs in order to blossom – because without persistence, love has no stamina. Love is not the affection of a millisecond, a mere whim, that is offered now and withdrawn in annoyance or distraction a moment later. Real love is abiding and lasting and faithful – thus it must have persistence.

But the most obvious creation of love is happiness, for happiness cannot be where love is not – they are constant companions. Without happiness, love is an impostor. If what you do does not make you happy, re-examine it, reconceptualize it, redo it, until it is animated by affection.

Love also created courage so that you might never be thwarted by fear. Without courage, love is afraid to be born. Courage is the great facilitator: it makes possible all virtues, including love. You need it to speak when your colleagues are misguided; you need it to be kind when the world would be cruel; you need it to be yourself when conformity is foolish. You need courage to stand amidst breaking worlds when your concept of self is most endangered. You need it to trust others and to love others – because trusting and loving make you vulnerable, and that may make you afraid. It takes courage to be honest, to pursue the truth, even to be reliable under adverse conditions.

Self-evolvement is not for cowards. A study of the world's enlightened beings shows that they are truly courageous – and that they are love itself, and love's family of enabling, ennobling and expanding virtues.

David C. Jones

# Prologue

We bury love; forgetfulness grows over it like grass. That is a thing to weep for, not the dead.

*Alexander Smith*

A society without love is like a land without rivers....

*J. Krishnamurti*

Love is the only bow on life's dark cloud. It is the morning and the evening star. It shines upon the babe, and sheds its radiance on the quiet tomb. It is the Mother of Art, inspirer of poet, patriot and philosopher. It is the air and light to tired souls – builder of every home, kindler of every fire on every hearth. It was the first to dream of immortality. It fills the world with melody – for music is the voice of love. Love is the magician, the enchanter that changes worthless things to joy, and makes right-royal kings and queens of common clay. It is the perfume of that wondrous flower, the heart, and without that sacred passion, that divine swoon, we are less than beasts; but with it, earth is heaven and we are gods.

*Robert G. Ingersoll*

## Growing in Silence

Silence is painful; but in silence things take form, and we must wait and watch. In us, in our secret depth, lies the knowing element which sees and hears that which we do not see nor hear. All our perceptions, all the things we have done, all that we are today, dwelt once in that knowing, silent depth, that treasure chamber in the soul. And we are more than we think. We are more than we know. That which is more than we think and know is always seeking and adding to itself while we are doing nothing – or think we are doing nothing. But to be conscious of what is going on in our depth is to help it along. When sub-conscious-ness becomes consciousness, the seeds in our winter-clad selves turn to flowers, and the silent life in us sings with all its might.

*Kahlil Gibran*

The center of the universe, as far as your perceptions are concerned, lies in yourself. Never belittle your potential, for everything you can ever know begins with self-acceptance and develops through self-understanding.

*J. Donald Walters*

I pray Thee, O God, that I may be beautiful within.

*Socrates*

There is only one Religion, the Religion of Love.
There is only one Caste, the Caste of Humanity.
There is only one Language, the Language of the
   Heart.

A heart devoid of Love is an altar plunged into
   darkness.

The Grace of God cannot be won through the gymna-
sium of reason, the contortions of Yoga or the denials of
asceticism. Love alone can win it, Love that needs no
requital, Love that knows no bargaining, Love that is
unwavering. Love alone can overcome obstacles, however
many and mighty.

Love cannot be cultivated by reading guidebooks and
made-easies and learning the steps by rote. It has to begin
with a great yearning for the Light and unbearable agony
to escape from Darkness.

*Sathya Sai Baba*

## Love's Promise

If you want to touch the other shore badly enough, barring an impossible situation, you will. But if your desire is diluted for any reason, you will never make it.

*Diana Nyad*

"I must be in the right mood to examine myself fruitfully," a seeker suggested.

"You must be serious, intent, truly interested," Master Nisargadatta Maharaj replied. "You must be full of goodwill for yourself.

"The desire to find the self will be surely fulfilled, provided you want nothing else. But you must be honest with yourself and really want nothing else. If in the meantime you want many other things and are engaged in their pursuit, your main purpose may be delayed until you grow wiser and cease being torn between contradictory urges. Go within, without swerving, without ever looking outward."

"What can make me love?" asked the seeker.

"You are love itself – when you are not afraid."

# The Faces of Love

There can be no secret in life and morals, because Nature has provided that every beautiful thought you know and every precious sentiment you feel will shine out of your face, so that all who are great enough may see, know, understand, appreciate and appropriate. You keep things only by giving them away.

*Elbert Hubbard*

Love is very patient and kind, never jealous or envious, never boastful or proud, never haughty or selfish or rude. Love does not demand its own way. It is not irritable or touchy. It does not hold grudges and will hardly even notice when others do it wrong. It is never glad about injustice, but rejoices whenever truth wins out. If you love someone you will be loyal to him no matter what the cost. You will always believe in him, always expect the best of him, and always stand your ground in defending him.

*St. Paul, The Living Bible*

## Love's Attendants

> Without patience
> Love has no time.
> Without persistence
> it has no stamina.
> Without happiness
> it is an impostor.
> Without courage
> it is afraid to be born.
> Without mercy
> it is stillborn.

*DCJ*

## Love is Absorption in the Now

If you observe a really happy man you will find him building a boat, writing a symphony, educating his son, growing double dahlias in his garden, or looking for dinosaur eggs in the Gobi desert. He will not be searching for happiness as if it were a collar button that has rolled under the radiator. He will not be striving for it as a goal in itself. He will have become aware that he is happy in the course of living life twenty-four crowded hours of the day.

*W. Beran Wolfe*

Life isn't a matter of milestones but of moments.

*Rose Fitzgerald Kennedy*

## Love is Adaptable

Develop adaptability. Keep your love fluid, that it fill whatever vessel life places before you.

*J. Donald Walters*

## *Love is Amiable*

There is nothing so hygienic as friendship. Hell is a separation, and Heaven is only going home to your friends.

Don't be a villager – be universal, no matter where you live.

*Elbert Hubbard*

A friend is a gift you give to yourself.

*Robert Louis Stevenson*

"A friend of mine used to have horrible dreams night after night," a seeker told the Master. "Going to sleep would terrorize him. Nothing could help him."

"Company of the truly good would help him," answered Nisargadatta Maharaj.

"Life itself is a nightmare," the questioner persisted.

"Noble friendship is the supreme remedy for all ills, physical and mental," said the Master.

To love a friend intensely, yet with pure detachment; to let him be equally or even more a friend of others; to expect no affection, while being duly appreciative of whatever affection is given; to think of how one can help, rather than of what gratification one can get; to be constant in friendship and unselfish helpfulness; to bring to the physical level the beautiful, selfless spirit of the higher planes – this is the ideal love.

*N. Sri Ram*

# Love is Attentive

The first duty of love is to listen.

Paul Tillich

Listening is not something that comes naturally; it is an acquired art. For most of us, listening, whether in a social conversation or around the table at a conference, is just a pause we feel obliged to grant a speaker until we again have a chance to air our own opinions. This is not real listening in any sense of the word. Listening is not a passive activity during which we let our own thoughts intrude upon what someone else is saying. To actively listen to another person requires willpower, concentration and great mental effort.

*J.C. Penney*

Spend more time in listening to others. To speak excessively is anesthetizing. Listen for the thoughts and the vibrations behind people's words.

*J. Donald Walters*

## Love is Beauty-filled

There is inward beauty only when you feel real love for people and for all the things of the earth; and with that love there comes a tremendous sense of consideration, watchfulness, patience. You may have perfect technique, as a singer or a poet, you may know how to paint or put words together, but without this creative beauty inside, your talent will have very little significance.

*J. Krishnamurti*

You are infinitely beautiful when you give without one single thought of asking or taking.

*N. Sri Ram*

Beauty is reality seen through the eyes of love.

*Evelyn Underhill*

## Love is Brotherly and Sisterly

To have courage without pugnacity,
To have conviction without bigotry,
To have charity without condescension,
To have faith without credulity,
To have love of humanity without mere
    sentimentality,
To have meekness with power
And emotion with sanity – That is brotherhood.

*Charles E. Hughes*

## Love is Cheerful

Cheerfulness is the atmosphere in which all things thrive.

*Jean Paul Richter*

## Love is Compassionate

Tell me how much you know of the sufferings of your fellow men, and I will tell how much you have loved them.

*Helmut Thielicke*

The dew of compassion is a tear.

*Lord Byron*

## Love is Complimentary

If you want children to improve, let them overhear the nice things you say about them to others.

*Haim Ginott*

## Love is Constructive Criticism

The trouble with most of us is that we would rather be ruined by praise than saved by criticism.

*Norman Vincent Peale*

Instead of criticizing others and finding faults with the actions of others, subject yourself to vigilant scrutiny, understand yourself well, and correct your own faults. Do not be like the dancer who blamed the drummer for her wrong steps.

*Sathya Sai Baba*

## Love is Courageous Application

Every great improvement has come after repeated failures. Virtually nothing comes out right the first time. Failures, repeated failures, are finger posts on the road to achievement.

*Charles Kettering*


## Love is Courteous

Everyone is polite to a chief, but a man of manners is polite to everyone.

*Kongo proverb*

## Love is Discreet

Many truths are best not recalled, especially those that only degrade people.

*Maxim Gorky*

Among my most prized possessions are words that I have never spoken.

*Orson Rega Card*

## Love is Enthusiastic

The secret of genius is to carry the spirit of the child into old age, which means never losing your enthusiasm.

*Aldous Huxley*

## Love is Faith-filled

Faith is the bird that sings when the dawn is still dark.

*Rabindranath Tagore*

## Love is Generous

No person was ever honored for what he received. Honor has been the reward for what he gave.

*Calvin Coolidge*

When you cease to make a contribution you begin to die.

*Eleanor Roosevelt*

## Love is Gentle

The world does not require so much to be informed as reminded.

*Hannah More*


## Love is Godly

The best way to know God is to love many things.

*Vincent Van Gogh*


## Love is Grateful

Though it is never demanded by love, gratitude is the only lens through which we see love, for it is the sure sign that love has been recognized.

Gratitude is also love's natural response to love.

*DCJ*

## Love is Healing

Nothing in the world is holier than helping one who asks for help.

*Supplements to A Course in Miracles, Psychotherapy, 23*

We can be cured of depression in only 14 days, if every day we will try to think of how we can be helpful to others.

*Alfred Adler*

## Love is Honorable

He who is the slowest in making a promise is the most faithful in the performance of it.

*Jean Jacques Rousseau*

## Love is Hopeful

He is the best physician who is the most ingenious inspirer of hope.

*Samuel Taylor Coleridge*

Hope is the only bee that makes honey without flowers.

*Robert G. Ingersoll*

## Love is Hospitable

Who practices hospitality entertains God Himself.

*The Talmud*

## Love is Immortal

All that is not given is lost.

*Indian proverb*

Talk not of wasted affection;
Affection was never wasted.

*Henry Wadsworth Longfellow*

## Love is Inspiring

By appreciation we make excellence in others our own property.

*Voltaire*

## Love is Intimate

### The First Kiss

. . . A word uttered by four lips making the heart a throne, and love a sovereign, and fulfillment a crown.

*Kahlil Gibran*

## Love is Jovial

Honest good humor is the oil and wine of a merry meeting, and there is no jovial companionship equal to that where the jokes are rather small and the laughter abundant.

*Washington Irving*

All who would win joy, must share it; happiness was born a twin.

*Lord Byron*

We cannot really love anybody with whom we never laugh.

*Agnes Repplier*

## *Love is Kind*

If someone tells you a story about another, should you repeat it? Only after it passes through three gates, advises <u>The Arabian</u>. The first – is it true? The second, is it needful? The third and narrowest – is it kind? If it passes all three, you may speak it.

*DCJ*

The entire Roman government could not have roused unkindness in Christ.

*Paramahansa Yogananda*

## Love is Living

You will find as you look back upon your life, that the moments when you have really lived are the moments when you have done things in the spirit of love.

*Henry Drummond*

## *Love is Merciful*

[M]ercy is a quality of growth. You should realize that there is a great reward of personal satisfaction in being first just, next fair, then patient, then kind. And then, on that foundation, if you choose and have it in your heart, you can take the next step and really show mercy; but you cannot exhibit mercy in and of itself. These steps must be traversed; otherwise there can be no genuine mercy. There may be patronage, condescension, or charity – even pity – but not mercy.

*The URANTIA Book, 315*

## Love is Non-intrusive

Do not go out of your way to do good, but do good whenever it comes your way.

*Elbert Hubbard*

We can reach only those who are ready to be reached. We can do nothing with those who are not ready to receive either the truths of the spirit or its sublime power.

*Silver Birch*

It is not good to give one's advice unasked.

*Janet Erskine Stuart*

Any man who reforms himself has contributed his full share towards the reformation of his neighbor.

*Norman Douglas*

## *Love is Non-judgmental*

Charity sees the need, not the cause.

*German proverb*

You have no idea of the tremendous release and deep peace that comes from meeting yourself and your brothers totally without judgment.

*A Course in Miracles,* text, 47

## *Love is Non-possessive*

I appreciate whatever God gives me, but I don't miss it when it is gone. Someone once gave me a beautiful coat and hat, an expensive outfit. Then began my worry. I had to be concerned about not tearing or soiling it. It made me uncomfortable. I said, "Lord, why did you give me this bother?" One day I was to lecture in Trinity Hall here in Los Angeles. When I arrived at the hall and started to remove my coat, the Lord told me. "Take away your belongings from the pockets." I did so. When I returned to the cloak-room after my lecture, the coat was gone. I was angry, and someone said, "Never mind, we will get you another coat." I replied, "I am not angry because I lost the coat, but because whoever took it didn't take the hat that matches it, too."

*Paramahansa Yogananda*

## Love is Non-violent

He who cherishes the values of culture cannot fail to be a pacifist.

*Albert Einstein*

## Love is Patient

How poor are they who have not patience! What wound did ever heal but by degrees.

*William Shakespeare*

## Love Generates Perfection

It is in a state of love that all perfections arise; it is the state in which there is no self-centeredness.

*N. Sri Ram*

## Love is Power

Life is a search for power. To have power you must have life, and life in abundance. And life in abundance comes only through great love.

*Elbert Hubbard*

Acceptance and understanding can be expected only from the strong.

*Leo Buscaglia*

## *Love is Respect*

The commandment to honor one's parents has come down through the ages, but to honor thy daughter and thy son is a commandment no less imperative. Do not clip the wings of their idealism for the fear of the hardships that they may encounter.

*Lillian Wald*

There can be no real freedom without the freedom to fail.

*Eric Hoffer*

"When one looks round, one is appalled by the volume of unnecessary suffering that is going on," said a questioner. "People who should be helped are not getting help. Imagine a big hospital ward full of incurables, tossing and moaning. Were you given the authority to kill them all and end their torture, would you not do so?"

"I would leave it to them to decide," said Nisargadatta Maharaj.

## Love Sees the Best

Sadness is but a wall between two gardens.

*Kahlil Gibran*

Every human being has at least one good quality. I look for that when I meet a man and then try to compliment him on it.

*Will Rogers*

Make the most of the best and the least of the worst.

*Robert Louis Stevenson*

Accept from others only what you choose to accept: their good suggestions but not their insistence on them; their constructive criticisms but not their anger.

*J. Donald Walters*

## *Love is Self-Appreciation*

Don't be afraid to follow your own star, though it shine for no one else.

*J. Donald Walters*

No man who is occupied in doing a very difficult thing, and doing it very well, ever loses his self-respect.

*George Bernard Shaw*

## *Love Encourages Self-Inquiry*

One secret of progress is self-analysis. Introspection is a mirror in which to see recesses of your mind that otherwise would remain hidden from you. Diagnose your failures and sort out your good and bad tendencies. Analyze what you are, what you wish to become, and what shortcomings are impeding you.

True self-analysis is the greatest art of progress.

Write down your thoughts and aspirations daily. Find out what you are — not what you imagine you are! — because you want to make yourself what you ought to be. Most people don't change because they don't see their own faults.

*Paramahansa Yogananda*

## Love is Service

Service is the coin of the spirit. There is no religion higher than service. It is noble to serve. If you cannot serve where you would like, then serve where the opportunity comes.

*Silver Birch*

In being of spiritual, mental and material service to others, you will find your own needs fulfilled. As you forget self in service to others, you will find that, without seeking it, your own cup of happiness will be full.

*Paramahansa Yogananda*

## Love is Sharing

We are each of us angels with only one wing, and we can fly only by embracing one another.

*Luciano de Crescenzo*

## Love is Tactful

We have read your manuscript with boundless delight. If we were to publish your paper, it would be impossible for us to publish any work of lower standard. And as it is unthinkable that in the next thousand years we shall see its equal, we are, to our regret, compelled to return your divine composition, and to beg you a thousand times to overlook our short sight and timidity.

*Rejection slip from a Chinese economic journal*

## Love is Timely

You cannot do a kindness too soon, for you never know how soon it will be too late.

*Ralph Waldo Emerson*


## Love is Understanding

Home is not where you live but where they understand you.

*Christian Morgenstern*

That is the extraordinary thing about love: it is the only quality that brings a total comprehension of the whole of existence.

*J. Krishnamurti*

## *Love is Venturesome, Infinitely Unfolding, and Ever Welcoming*

Anchorage is what most people pray for, when what they really need is God's great open sea.

*Elbert Hubbard*

I wanted a perfect ending. . . . Now I've learned, the hard way, that some poems don't rhyme, and some stories don't have a clear beginning, middle and end. Life is about not knowing, having to change, taking the moment and making the best of it, without knowing what's going to happen next. Delicious ambiguity.

*Gilda Radner*

And the fruits of the divine spirit which are yielded in the lives of spirit-born and God-knowing mortals are: loving service, unselfish devotion, courageous loyalty, sincere fairness, enlightened honesty, undying hope, confiding trust, merciful ministry, unfailing goodness, forgiving tolerance, and enduring peace.

*The URANTIA Book*, 2054

## A Test

The best index to a person's character is (a) how he treats people who can't do him any good, and (b) how he treats people who can't fight back.

*Abigail Van Buren*

# What Only Looks Like Love

## Patronizing Love

You who would be your brother's keeper, have you asked him what he wants? If he says, "nothing," will you tell him what he <u>should</u> want? And if he says something, will you weaken him by doing it for him?

*DCJ*

## Exclusive Love

Do not keep your kindness in water-tight compartments. If it runs over a bit t'will do no harm.

*Elbert Hubbard*

## Inconsistent Love

I have seen gross intolerance shown in support of tolerance.

*Samuel Taylor Coleridge*

## Overwhelmed Love

. . . Overmuch sympathy and pity may degenerate into serious emotional instability. . . .

*The URANTIA Book, 1673*

## Possessive Love

Affection must never be so overwhelming that it overrides another's willingness to be loved.

*DCJ*

## Divorced Love

The love of the past is often but the hatred of the present.

*Dorion*

## Uncomforting Love

Give your friends strength and understanding in their sorrows, but don't share their grief so deeply that you intensify it.

*J. Donald Walters*

## Weeping Love

Exaggerated sensitiveness is an expression of the feeling of inferiority.

*Alfred Adler*

# What is Not Love

## Fear

Your mind is like a bird that has been locked in a cage
for many years. It fears liberty, yet freedom is its birthright.

*Paramahansa Yogananda*

. . . No one reaches love with fear beside him.

*A Course in Miracles*, text, 422

*FEAR*
is one of the major cornerstones
of the karmic condition.
It speaks
to the distrust of eternal love.

It is a disbelief
in yourself.
It is an extreme perversion
of truth and light
and love,
which is precisely what your world
is all about –
the healing
of the extreme distortions
of truth and light
and love.

*Emmanuel*

As long as you are afraid of anyone or anything, there can be no happiness. There can be no happiness as long as you are afraid of your parents, your teachers, afraid of not passing examinations, afraid of not making progress, of not getting nearer to the Master, nearer to truth, or of not being approved of, patted on the back. But if you are really not afraid of anything, then you will find – when you wake up of a morning, or when you are walking alone – that suddenly a strange thing happens: uninvited, unsolicited, unlooked-for, that which may be called love, truth, happiness, is suddenly there.

*J.Krishnamurti*

## Hate

The formula for hate: Keep your eye on each other's deficiencies.

*Elbert Hubbard*

There is no greater hatred in the world than the hatred of ignorance for knowledge.

*Galileo Galilei*

Hatred is a coward's revenge for being intimidated.

*George Bernard Shaw*

By heaping hatred upon hatred, or giving hate in return for love, you not only increase your enemy's hostility toward you, you poison your system, physically as well as emotionally, with your own venom.

*Paramahansa Yogananda*

# Anger

Anger. A wind which blows out the lamp of the mind.

*Robert G. Ingersoll*

Have you noticed how angry you sometimes get with a friend of yours? . . . You are expecting something from him, and when that expectation is not fulfilled, you are disappointed – which means, really, that inwardly psychologically you are depending on that person. So wherever there is psychological dependence, there must be frustration; and frustration inevitably breeds anger, bitterness, jealousy and various other forms of conflict.

*J. Krishnamurti*

Anger is an inner recognition of impotence.

*J. Donald Walters*

## Assertive Philanthropy

Why push the Truth down unwilling throats? It cannot be done, anyhow. Without a receiver what can the giver do?

*Nisargadatta Maharaj*

Don't impose your ideas on others. Offer them.

*J. Donald Walters*

You cannot give anything to those who are not ready to receive it.

*Silver Birch*

## Oppression

You can't hold a man down without staying down with him.

*Booker T. Washington*

## Bigotry

The mind of the bigot is like the pupil of the eye. The more light you pour upon it, the more it will contract.

*Oliver Wendell Holmes, Jr.*

## Envy

Envy is deadly poison; it will contaminate character, ruin health and rob you of peace. . . . Like a pest that destroys growing crops, envy enters slowly and spreads quickly. So even in small matters you must be vigilant; do not become envious.

*Sathya Sai Baba*

## Doubt

Our doubts are traitors
And make us lose the good we oft might win
By fearing to attempt.

*William Shakespeare*

## Resentment

He who cannot forgive breaks the bridge over which
he himself must pass.

*George Herbert*

## Hurtfulness

No teacher of God but must learn – and fairly early in
his training – that harmfulness completely obliterates his
function from his awareness. It will make him confused,
fearful, angry and suspicious.

*A Course in Miracles, manual, 13*

Contempt is the subtlest form of revenge.

*Baltasar Gracian*

## Selfishness

Self is love-less-ness; Love is self-less-ness. Self gets and forgets; love gives and forgives. Love can never entertain the idea of revenge, for it sees all others as oneself. When the tongue is hurt by the teeth, do you seek vengeance against the wrong-doer?

*Sathya Sai Baba*

Naturally, selfishness is always destructive. Desire and fear, both are self-centered states. Between desire and fear anger arises, with anger hatred, with hatred passion for destruction. War is hatred in action, organized and equipped with all the instruments of death.

*Nisargadatta Maharaj*

## Mistrust

At the gate where suspicion enters, love goes out.

*English proverb*

## Separation

Alone, one withers.

*Johann August Strindberg*

## Poisoning Faith

It is wrong to undermine the faith of another and disturb your own. Faith is a plant of slow growth; its roots go deep into the heart.

*Sathya Sai Baba*

## Apathy

The Devil was once auctioning his spiritual poisons to apprentices – one by one he handed out greed, hate, pride, envy, lust, cynicism and suspicion. But the apprentice who purchased suspicion immediately suspected the Devil of withholding something.

Indeed he was.

"It is my most potent weapon," the Devil admitted, allowing the apprentice just a glimpse of the label, which read – INDIFFERENCE.

# Corrupted Love

Love is the highest motivation which man may utilize in his universe ascent. But love, divested of truth, beauty and goodness, is only a sentiment, a philosophic distortion, a psychic illusion, a spiritual deception.

*The URANTIA Book, 2096*

Your giving is weakened by any form of regret over the giving – because regret is a wish that you had never given at all. The more intense the wish, the tinier the gift. And the regret can take different forms – one, that whatever was given is lost forever; others, that the receiver will not appreciate the gift, or will not use it "properly," or will not return it somehow, or was not worthy of it in the first place.

*DCJ*

Gifts should be handed not thrown.

*Danish proverb*

Even your enthusiasm, the cream of aliveness, will sour if you insist that it be someone else's ideal. Share your aliveness and laud the enthusiasms of others, yes, but do not demand that your interests be theirs.

*DCJ*

A heavy guilt rests upon us for what the whites of all nations have done to the colored peoples. When we do good to them, it is not benevolence – it is atonement.

*Albert Schweitzer*

## A Test

I can see myself exactly as I am in the mirror of my relationship with others. I can observe how I talk to people: most politely to those who I think can give me something, and rudely or contemptuously to those who cannot. I am attentive to those I am afraid of. I get up when important people come in, but when the servant enters I pay no attention. So, by observing myself in relationship, I have found out how falsely I respect people, have I not?

*J. Krishnamurti*

## How to Love

You cannot truly love your fellows by a mere act of the will. Love is only born of thoroughgoing understanding of your neighbor's motives and sentiments.

*The URANTIA Book*, 1098

# Final Missives

## Love's Miracle

Love teaches even asses to dance.

*French proverb*

## Love's Fury

Do not use a hatchet to remove a fly from your friend's forehead.

*Chinese proverb*

## Love's Hedge

Why is it better to love than to be loved? It is surer!

*Sacha Guitry*

## Love's Duration

Love is eternal, as long as it lasts.

*Vinicius de Moralis*

## Love's Problem

Every man wants a woman to appeal to his better side, his nobler instincts and his higher nature – and another woman to help him forget them.

*Helen Rowland*

## Compensations

One thing nice about egoists: they don't talk about other people.

*Lucilee Harper*

Charity suffereth long – and so does the man who tries to live on it.

*Elbert Hubbard*

The surest cure for vanity is loneliness.

*Thomas Wolfe*

# Epilogue

You are a spark of an Eternal Flame. You can hide the spark, but you can never destroy it.

*Paramahansa Yogananda*

There is a vastness beyond the farthest reaches of the mind. That vastness is my home; that vastness is myself. And that vastness is also love.

*Nisargadatta Maharaj*

Love is a fruit in season at all times, and within reach of every hand.

*Mother Teresa*

Do what you love. Know your own bone; gnaw at it, bury it, unearth it and gnaw it still.

*Henry David Thoreau*

With a sweet tongue and kindness, you can drag an elephant by a hair.

*Persian proverb*

How far you go in life depends on your being tender with the young, compassionate with the aged, sympathetic with the striving and tolerant of the weak and strong. Because someday in life you will have been all of these.

*George Washington Carver*

Love is the only thing that we can carry with us when we go, and it makes the end so easy.

*Louisa May Alcott*